MINECRAFT

MOJANG

EGMONT

We bring stories to life

First published in Great Britain 2014 by Egmont UK Limited
The Yellow Building, 1 Nicholas Road
London W11 4AN

Written by Stephanie Milton, with help from Paul Soares Jr, FyreUK and CNB Minecraft.
Designed by Andrea Philpots
Concept design by Steffan Glynn
Illustrations by Theo Cordner and FyreUK
Production by Louis Harvey and Caroline Hancock
© 2014 Notch Development AB

'Minecraft' is a trademark of Notch Development AB

◪MOJANG

ISBN 978 1 4052 6841 7
55908/9
Printed in Italy

MIX
Paper from
responsible sources
FSC® C018306

Egmont is passionate about helping to preserve the world's remaining ancient forests.
We only use paper from legal and sustainable forest sources.

This book is made from paper certified by the Forest Stewardship Council® (FSC®),
an organisation dedicated to promoting responsible management of forest resources.
For more information on the FSC, please visit www.fsc.org. To learn more about
Egmont's sustainable paper policy, please visit www.egmont.co.uk/ethical

**Stay safe online. Any website addresses listed in this book are correct at the
time of going to print. However, Egmont is not responsible for content hosted by
third parties. Please be aware that online content can be subject to change and
websites can contain content that is unsuitable for children. We advise that all
children are supervised when using the internet.**

The publishers have used every endeavour to trace copyright owners and secure appropriate
permissions for materials reproduced in this book. In case of any unintentional omission,
the publishers will be pleased to hear from the relevant copyright owner.

MINECRAFT

MOJANG

COMBAT HANDBOOK

CONTENTS

INTRODUCTION

WELCOME TO THE OFFICIAL MINECRAFT COMBAT HANDBOOK. IT'S ESSENTIAL READING FOR WARRIORS!

This book is packed with tips from Minecraft experts like master builders FyreUK, YouTube sensation Paul Soares Jr and redstone expert CNB Minecraft.

Read on to learn how to defend your home, build a fort, fight monsters, set traps, thrive in PVP (player versus player) mode, evade death in the Nether and battle the dreaded ender dragon in the End.

With the help of this handbook, you'll be a Minecraft warrior of the highest order in no time!

TIP: STAYING SAFE ONLINE
Playing Minecraft on multiplayer servers is great fun! Here are a few simple rules to help you stay safe and keep the world of Minecraft a great place to spend time:

- Never give out your real name – don't use it as your username.
- Never give out any of your personal details.
- Never tell anybody which school you go to or how old you are.
- Never tell anybody your password except a parent or guardian.

BASIC WEAPONS

Weapons are items used to deal damage to other players or mobs, or to block attacks. There are several basic weapons that should be at the core of any warrior's arsenal.

SWORD

A sword's sharpness makes it the best weapon to use during close-range/melee combat. A sword can be crafted from 1 stick plus 2 pieces of wood, cobblestone, smelted iron, smelted gold or diamond gems.

Diamond swords are by far the most durable and will inflict the most damage, but diamond is one of the trickiest elements to find in Minecraft as it generates deep underground. If you don't have any diamonds, just craft a sword out of the strongest element you have to hand.

SWORD DURABILITY TABLE

MATERIAL	Wood	Stone	Iron	Gold	Diamond
DURABILITY	60	132	251	33	1562
DAMAGE	5	6	7	5	8
APPROX KILLS	15–24	39–66	87–138	8–13	624–1015
LIFETIME DAMAGE	150–240	396–660	878–1380	82–132	6248–10153

WOODEN SWORD RECIPE

A great starter weapon, but you'll soon need an upgrade.

COBBLESTONE SWORD RECIPE

Has a little more bite and will do until you can access rare ores.

IRON SWORD RECIPE

Now we're talking! An iron sword will last a good while.

GOLDEN SWORD RECIPE

A golden sword isn't very durable, but it's the easiest to enchant.

DIAMOND SWORD RECIPE

The ultimate fighting implement for the player who intends to dominate.

SWORD MAINTENANCE

You can rename and repair a sword on an anvil. Access your anvil and place the sword in the first slot, then either add a second sword to repair or change the text to rename. The cost in experience points will appear at the bottom.

ANVIL RECIPE

An anvil can be crafted from 3 iron blocks and 4 iron ingots.

REPAIR & NAME

Sword of Doom_

Enchantment Cost: 7

BASIC WEAPONS
... CONTINUED

BOW AND ARROW

The main advantage of a bow and arrow is that, unlike a sword, you can use it from a distance and keep out of range of your enemy's attack.

BOW RECIPE

A bow can be crafted from 3 sticks and 3 pieces of string.

Durability: **385**

ARROW RECIPE

Arrows can be crafted from flint (obtained by mining gravel), a stick and a feather (dropped by chickens when they die).

A fully charged bow and arrow can deal 9 points of damage per hit. To charge your bow, just hold down the use item button until it begins to shake. This will make the arrows go further and do maximum damage. It takes just 1 second to fully charge, which is very useful when you're in a fight.

DID YOU KNOW?

Bows can be enchanted with a variety of helpful effects such as unbreaking, punch and flame. Turn to pages 38–41 for more information on enchanting.

ENCHANT

DISPENSERS

As its name suggests, a dispenser is a mechanism that stores and dispenses items. It can be used to fire arrows, eggs, snowballs and splash potions at your opponents, and it can hold up to 9 stacks of 64 items.

DISPENSER RECIPE

A dispenser can be crafted from cobblestone, redstone dust and a bow.

LEVER RECIPE

Now connect it to a lever using redstone dust. A lever can be crafted from 1 cobblestone and a stick.

Access the dispenser then drag the required items into the 9 item slots that appear. Now you're all set to start using your dispenser.

Throw the lever to activate the dispenser and your ammunition of choice will be fired out. Just make sure it's pointed in the right direction.

BASIC WEAPONS
... CONTINUED

FLINT AND STEEL

This is a handy tool that allows you to make fire and can be used as a weapon against your enemies. Once crafted, select it in your hotbar and use it on a flammable block to set it alight. Aim for the block underneath your opponent, or a block directly in their path, and you'll soon get rid of them.

FLINT AND STEEL RECIPE

A flint and steel can be crafted from flint and an iron ingot.

LAVA BUCKET

A lava bucket can be used to damage several opponents at once as it allows you to place lava in their path or to drop it on top of them. Find some lava, select the bucket from your hotbar and use it on the lava to collect it. To place the lava, just use the bucket in the desired destination.

BUCKET RECIPE

You'll need 3 iron ingots to make a bucket in which to hold your lava.

 WARNING: You can easily set yourself or your surroundings on fire when using fire or lava. Keep a water bucket in your hotbar to put out any accidental fires.

TNT

Activate the TNT using a flint and steel, fire, a redstone current or another explosion in the near vicinity. If lighting with a flint and steel, make sure you get away quickly, or else you'll go BOOM along with the TNT!

TNT RECIPE

Craft a block of TNT from 5 gunpowder and 4 blocks of sand.

TNT: a simple yet effective way to annihilate an enemy base.

ARMOUR

Minecraft warriors need armour to protect themselves from attack and damage, especially when battling other players. A full set consists of a helmet, chestplate, trousers and boots.

You can craft armour from leather, gold, iron or diamond. Chainmail armour can sometimes be acquired through villager trading, or if a mob drops it when it dies. These substances offer varying degrees of protection.

HELMET RECIPE

Craft a helmet from 5 units of your chosen material.

CHESTPLATE RECIPE

A chestplate can be crafted from 8 units.

TROUSERS RECIPE

Trousers can be crafted from 7 units.

BOOTS RECIPE

Craft a pair of boots from 4 units.

Leather   Gold   Chainmail   Iron   Diamond

Armour will protect you from the following forms of damage:

 Mob attacks   Arrows   Explosions

 Other players   Fire and lava   Cacti

DEFENCE POINTS

A defence point is equal to half a chestplate in your armour bar. The more defence points your armour has, the more damage it will absorb over its lifetime. For example, a complete set of diamond armour will protect you from 80% of damage, compared to a complete set of iron armour which will protect you from only 60%.

DEFENCE POINTS TABLE

TYPE	FULL SET OF ARMOUR	HELMET	CHEST	LEGS	BOOTS
Leather	👕👕👕👕	👕	👕👕	👕	👕
Gold	👕👕👕👕👕	👕	👕👕👕	👕👕	👕
Chain	👕👕👕👕👕👕	👕	👕👕👕	👕👕	👕
Iron	👕👕👕👕👕👕👕	👕	👕👕👕	👕👕👕	👕
Diamond	👕👕👕👕👕👕👕👕👕👕	👕👕	👕👕👕👕	👕👕👕	👕👕

 DID YOU KNOW? You can dye leather armour by crafting it with a dye of your choice. Just add the item of armour to your crafting area along with the dye.

 TIP: It's a good idea to keep a spare set of armour in your inventory, especially if you're playing in PVP mode. That way, if your current armour is destroyed, you can quickly replace it and get back into battle.

MOB COMBAT

Fighting hostile monsters is the best way to kit yourself out with supplies for future combat! Let's start with the Overworld mobs before venturing to the Nether and the End.

SILVERFISH

HEALTH POINTS: 8 ♥♥♥♥

ATTACK STRENGTH: 1 ♦

ATTACK METHOD: Will run or jump towards you and inflict damage by touching you and by pushing you around. When 1 silverfish is attacked, more may awaken nearby and you may easily find yourself swarmed.

SPAWNS: From monster eggs/spawners found in strongholds. Rarely, underground in extreme hills biomes when a silverfish block is broken.

VULNERABLE TO: Lava Gravel

DO

Try building a 2-block high column to stand on and attack the silverfish safely from above.

DON'T

Use splash potions. This will result in you being swarmed by silverfish.

SPIDER

HEALTH POINTS: 16 ♡♡♡♡♡♡♡♡

ATTACK STRENGTH: 2-3 ♡ – ♡◖

ATTACK METHOD: Will leap towards you and hit you, inflicting damage until you die. Only hostile in low light levels. Once hostile they will remain so, even in daylight.

SPAWNS: In the Overworld in light levels of 7 or less.

VULNERABLE TO: Lava Cacti TNT

Fire Falling

USEFUL DROPS:

0-2 string, which can be used to make a bow.

0-1 spider eyes which can be used in potions.

DO

Try to get to higher ground than the spider. This will allow you to attack it repeatedly, preventing it from jumping up to your level.

DON'T

Let the spider have the high ground. This will give the spider the perfect opportunity to pounce on you from above.

SLIME

HEALTH POINTS: Large: 16 ♡♡♡♡♡♡♡♡ Medium: 4 ♡♡
Tiny: 1 ♡

ATTACK STRENGTH: Large: 4 ♡♡ Medium: 2 ♡ Tiny: 0

ATTACK METHOD: Will hop towards you and bump into you repeatedly, inflicting damage until you die.

SPAWNS: Below level 40 in specific chunks, at any light level. In swamp biomes between levels 51 and 69, in light levels of 8 or less.

VULNERABLE TO: Lava Cacti TNT

Fire 🔥 Falling 📦 Water 💧

USEFUL DROPS: ◯ Tiny slime drop 0–2 slimeballs, which can be used to make magma cream for potions.

DO

Lead them to water. Slimes can't swim and will drown if they can't hop out. They also burn in lava so try forcing them into some.

DON'T

Get yourself cornered by a swarm of slimes in a cave. They will soon deal enough damage to overpower you in a restricted space.

CREEPER

HEALTH POINTS: 20 ♡♡♡♡♡♡♡♡♡♡

ATTACK STRENGTH: 49 (regular) ♡ ✕24.5
and 97 (charged) ♡ ✕48.5

ATTACK METHOD: Runs at you and explodes in your face.

SPAWNS: In the Overworld in areas with a light level of 7 or less, but not on transparent blocks like glass. They don't die when the sun rises.

VULNERABLE TO: Lava Cacti

TNT Fire Falling Diamond Sword Bow and arrows

WHO TO TAKE: Cat Ocelot

Ocelots and tamed cats wouldn't hurt a fly, but will send creepers running for the hills.

USEFUL DROPS: Creepers drop 0–2 pieces of gunpowder, which you can use to make TNT and fire charges.

DO	DON'T
Keep a safe distance to stay out of range of their explosion. Attack with a bow and arrows before resorting to melee weapons.	Get too close, especially if you hear a hissing sound. Try to avoid close-quarters combat, or you may be blown to pieces.

SKELETON

HEALTH POINTS: 20 ♡♡♡♡♡♡♡♡♡♡

ATTACK STRENGTH: 2-6 ♡ - ♡♡♡

ATTACK METHOD: Will shoot at you with a bow and arrows.

SPAWNS: In the Overworld in areas with a light level of 7 or less, but not on transparent blocks like glass or half blocks.

VULNERABLE TO: Lava 🟧 Cacti 🟩 TNT 🟥

Fire 🔥 Falling ⚔️ Daylight ⬜ Splash potion of

healing 🧪

USEFUL DROPS: 🏹 0-2 arrows Their bow (rarely - may be enchanted) Random armour (rarely, if equipped - may be enchanted)

DO

Use its own weapon against it and shoot it from a distance with a bow and arrows.

DON'T

Let it pick up any headgear. If it manages to grab a helmet or pumpkin it will become immune to sunlight.

ZOMBIE

HEALTH POINTS: 20 ♡♡♡♡♡♡♡♡♡♡

ATTACK STRENGTH: 2–9 ♡ – ♡♡♡♡♡

ATTACK METHOD: Will amble towards you and touch you to inflict damage until you die.

SPAWNS: In the Overworld in areas with a light level of 7 or less, but not on transparent blocks like glass.

VULNERABLE TO: Lava Cacti TNT

Fire Falling ⚔ Splash potion of healing 🧪

USEFUL DROPS: ⚔ Iron sword and random armour (rarely, if equipped) which can come in handy if you're short on supplies.

DO

Try to lure them out into the sunshine if they're still hanging around in the shade when day comes. They won't last long!

DON'T

Get stuck in a long corridor. And don't let a zombie pick up any headgear as this will prevent it from catching fire in the sunlight.

WITCH

HEALTH POINTS: 26 ♡♡♡♡♡♡♡♡
♡♡♡♡♡

ATTACK METHOD: Will throw splash potions of poison, weakness, harming and slowness at you.

SPAWNS: In dimly-lit areas, often in witch huts.

VULNERABLE TO: Splash potion of poison and instant damage (but they are 85% immune to these) Arrows

USEFUL DROPS: 0-6 gunpowder which can be used to make TNT, 0-6 spider eyes which can be used in potions, Potions (rarely)

DO

Use a bow and arrows to take a witch out, as the bow's range is further than the witch's splash potion range.

DON'T

Set a witch alight with lava or fire as they will drink a potion of fire resistance.

ENDERMAN

HEALTH POINTS: 40 ♡♡♡♡♡♡♡♡♡♡
♡♡♡♡♡♡♡♡♡♡

ATTACK STRENGTH: 4–10 ♡♡ – ♡♡♡♡♡

ATTACK METHOD: Will teleport towards you and hit you, inflicting damage until you die.

SPAWNS: In the Overworld in areas with a light level of 7 or less, and in large numbers in the End.

VULNERABLE TO: Lava Cacti TNT

Fire Falling Water

USEFUL DROPS: 0–1 ender pearls (needed to get to the End)

DO	DON'T
Run for the nearest body of water or lava and get your back up against a wall to stop them teleporting behind you. If endermen take damage from either water or lava, they will return to a neutral state.	Look directly at an enderman from the upper legs upwards – this will be taken as a sign of hostility.

COMBAT IN THE NETHER

The Nether is a hellish dimension which you can access by creating a Nether portal in the Overworld. It's worth the trip as you can pick up many useful items here that aren't available anywhere else.

You'll need a minimum of 10 blocks of obsidian to build a Nether portal. Once you've constructed the portal, use a flint and steel or a fire charge to activate it, and jump through!

NETHER PORTAL

A full nether portal can be crafted from 14 blocks of obsidian. If you're short on obsidian, save yourself 4 blocks and cut out the corners. It'll still work!

Before entering the Nether, equip yourself with the following:

 Enchanted armour

  Enchanted weapons

 Several stacks of cobblestone blocks to create safe paths and build a barrier to protect your Nether portal

 Flint and steel (you'll need this to relight your Nether portal if it's destroyed)

 Torches Food

 DID YOU KNOW? In the PC/Mac Edition, 1 block in the Nether equals 8 blocks in the Overworld, so you can use the Nether as a shortcut to travel quickly across long distances. As long as you can handle the danger, that is! In the Xbox 360 Edition the Nether is limited in size and 1 block equals 3 blocks in the Overworld. The Nether doesn't currently exist for the Pocket Edition.

GHAST

HEALTH POINTS: 10 ♡♡♡♡♡

ATTACK STRENGTH: 17 max ♡♡♡♡♡♡♡♡♥

ATTACK METHOD: Will shoot fireballs out of their mouths.

SPAWNS: In the Nether, in a space of at least 5 x 4 x 5 blocks.

VULNERABLE TO: Their own weapon. Give the ghast a taste of its own medicine and deflect those fireballs right back at them with one of your weapons.

USEFUL DROPS: 0-2 gunpowder, which can be used to make TNT, 0-1 ghast tears, which can be used in potions.

DO	DON'T
Try hooking a ghast with your fishing rod and drawing it in towards you so you can finish it off with a sword.	Underestimate the range of a ghast fireball. You'll be surprised by how far they can travel.

MAGMA CUBE

HEALTH POINTS: Large: 16 ♥♥♥♥♥♥♥♥ Medium:4 ♥♥
Tiny: 1 ♥

ATTACK STRENGTH: Large: 6 ♥♥♥ Medium: 4 ♥♥ Tiny: 3 ♥♥

ATTACK METHOD: Will hop towards you and bump into you, inflicting damage until you die.

SPAWNS: In the Nether.

VULNERABLE TO: Drowning in water.

USEFUL DROPS: Large and medium magma cubes drop 0-1 magma cream, which can be used in potions.

DO

Try to hit them while they're in the air. That way you might be able to knock them backwards over a ledge.

DON'T

Try to take on a large magma cube with just a sword. You'll get away with it for tiny and medium magma cubes, but not large.

BLAZE

HEALTH POINTS: 20 ♡♡♡♡♡♡♡♡♡♡

ATTACK STRENGTH: 3-9 ♡◐-♡♡♡♡◐

ATTACK METHOD: Will launch fireballs at you, or set itself on fire if close to you.

SPAWNS: In Nether fortresses.

VULNERABLE TO: Snowballs ◯ Water ▨

USEFUL DROPS: ✏ 0-1 blaze rods, which can be used in potions.

DO

Drink a potion of fire resistance to protect yourself, as all their attack methods involve fire. Once face to face with a blaze, use snowballs to weaken it then finish it off with your sword.

DON'T

Try to take them on with just a sword. Blazes can fly and deal damage from a distance, so they'll soon kill you if you try melee combat.

WITHER SKELETON

HEALTH POINTS: 20 ♡♡♡♡♡♡♡♡♡♡

ATTACK STRENGTH: 4-10 ♡♡ - ♡♡♡♡♡

ATTACK METHOD: Will hit you with their sword, at which point you'll be inflicted with the wither effect for 10 seconds. You'll know this has happened as your health bar will turn black and you'll be damaged over time due to its poison-like effect.

SPAWNS: Near Nether fortresses, in light levels of 7 or less.

VULNERABLE TO: Diamond swords with the sharpness, smite or looting enchantment.

USEFUL DROPS: Stone sword (rarely). Wither skeleton skulls (rarely).

DO	DON'T
Try to get yourself into a 2-block-high space, as the wither skeleton won't be able to follow you. This way, you can attack then move backwards to avoid retaliation.	Get too close. Wither skeletons rely on you being within range of their sword to attack you.

ZOMBIE PIGMAN

HEALTH POINTS: 20 ♡♡♡♡♡♡♡♡♡♡

ATTACK STRENGTH: 5-13
♡♡♦-♡♡♡♡♡♡♦

ATTACK METHOD: A zombie pigman is neutral until you attack. When provoked, it will hit you with its sword, inflicting damage until you die.

SPAWNS: In any 2-block-high space in the Nether.

VULNERABLE TO: Drowning in water. ▨

USEFUL DROPS: 🗡 Golden sword (rarely - may be enchanted). 🪙 Gold ingots (rarely), which can be used to craft gold armour and weapons.

DO

Attack from a distance, with an enchanted bow and arrows, and try to pick them off one-by-one.

DON'T

Attack one if several more are in the area. They will all turn on you if you do, and you could find yourself swarmed.

29

WITHER

The wither is a boss mob like the ender dragon (see pages 34-37). It's player-made and can be crafted from 4 blocks of soul sand arranged in a T shape, with 3 wither skeleton skulls on top. The last block you place must be a skull or the wither won't spawn.

HEALTH POINTS: 300 ♥ ✕150

ATTACK STRENGTH: 5-12 ♥♥♥ – ♥♥♥♥♥♥

ATTACK METHOD: Launches wither skulls, which will inflict the wither effect (a poison that can kill you) upon contact with players.

SPAWNS: In the Overworld, when a player creates one.

WEAPONS: Enchanted diamond sword combined with splash potions

 and an enchanted bow

VULNERABLE TO: Potions Weapons

WHO TO TAKE: Snow golems will attack the wither and distract it. To craft one, simply place a pumpkin on top of 2 vertically stacked snow blocks.

USEFUL DROPS: 1 Nether star, which can be used to make a beacon – a block that is both a strong light source and a source of power for players. If placed on a pyramid it gives selected buffs to players within a certain radius.

STRATEGY: Preparation, preparation, preparation! Don't even think about spawning a wither until you're wearing armour and have the right weapons.

Try to spawn the wither in a confined space, underground if possible to keep it away from your belongings.

Forget your potions of strength and instant healing – you're going to need them!

GETTING TO THE END

The End is a terrifying spit of land in the middle of a spacelike dimension known as the Void. It's almost completely barren, but is inhabited by endermen and the terrifying ender dragon.

If you can defeat the ender dragon you'll be rewarded handsomely, so it's well worth the trip. Whilst you're there you can collect End stone, which has a high blast resistance. To get there you'll need an End portal, and these are found in portal rooms within strongholds. To find your nearest stronghold, you're likely to need several eyes of ender, and then up to 12 more to activate it.

EYE OF ENDER RECIPE

Craft an eye of ender from an ender pearl and blaze powder (made from blaze rods dropped by blazes in the Nether).

1

Use your eye of ender and it will fly away from you into the air before dropping back to the ground. Follow it, pick it up and repeat. There's a 1 in 5 chance that the eye will shatter when it drops, which is why you need several.

2

Eventually the eye will keep falling onto the same spot of land. This is where you'll find the stronghold, and you'll need to dig underground to get in. Just remember the Number One Rule for Minecraft: never dig straight down or you could fall into the lava in the centre of the portal.

3

Once inside the stronghold, make your way to the End portal – a lava pool surrounded by End portal blocks. All 12 End portal blocks will need to be activated with eyes of ender before it will work.

4

When the portal is activated, jump through the centre and you'll find yourself in the End. Good luck!

THE ENDER DRAGON

Once you get to the End, be prepared for awesome adventure and some serious combat. The ender dragon is ferociously aggressive, and there's nowhere to hide ...

It's pretty dark in the End, so you might not spot the dragon immediately. But don't worry – the fearsome snarls and glowing purple eyes will soon alert you to its location. Plus it'll pounce as soon as it spots you.

ENDER DRAGON STATS

HEALTH POINTS: 200 ♥×100

ATTACK STRENGTH: 6–15 ♥♥♥ - ♥♥♥♥♥♥♥♥

ATTACK METHOD: Will dive towards you and hit you, inflicting damage until you die.

SPAWNS: In the End.

VULNERABLE TO: Not much. The Ender dragon is immune to lava, fire, water and enchantments and only takes damage from swords and arrows.

DROPS: TOP SECRET

TIP: Diamond armour will protect you from endermen as well as the dragon, and wearing a pumpkin head stops endermen from attacking if you look at them.

WARNING: Once in the End, you won't be able to get out alive unless you manage to defeat the ender dragon.

TNT

THE ENDER DRAGON
... CONTINUED

DID YOU KNOW?
In the Xbox 360 Edition, 2 of the ender crystals are surrounded by iron bars, so they'll be more difficult to destroy. Shooting them from a distance with a bow and arrows won't do the trick – you'll have to climb the obsidian pillars.

Before you even think about attacking the dragon, you need to destroy the ender crystals that sit on top of the obsidian pillars as these crystals will heal it.

Shoot them with arrows, snowballs or eggs until they explode. If you don't have any, use ladders to climb up to the top of the pillars.

Now for the difficult bit: defeating the ender dragon. Try shooting it with arrows and keep an eye on its health bar to check how close you are to finishing it off. **And what happens if you succeed? Well, we wouldn't want to give away the secret …**

 TIP: You can use a bed as a weapon in the End. Place it on the ground in front of you, and when the dragon gets near enough, use it as if you want to sleep, then jump back quickly. The bed will explode in the dragon's face, damaging its health.

ENCHANTING

Weapons and armour can be enchanted to improve their strength and performance and to give you a real edge over your opponent. There are several ways to enchant items.

USING AN ENCHANTMENT TABLE

An enchantment table is crafted from 4 obsidian blocks, 2 diamond gems and 1 book. Craft a book from 1 piece of leather (often dropped by cows when they die) and 3 pieces of paper (made from 3 pieces of sugar cane). You won't need the leather on the Xbox 360 or Pocket Editions.

PAPER RECIPE

BOOK RECIPE

ENCHANTMENT TABLE RECIPE

Access your enchantment table, then place the item you wish to enchant in the empty square and choose 1 of the 3 options that appears on the right. The options are written in the standard galactic alphabet so you won't know which one you're choosing until the item is enchanted. The numbers that appear to the right of the standard galactic alphabet text tell you how many experience points you'll have to pay.

ENCHANTING CONTINUED

COMBINING ITEMS ON AN ANVIL

An anvil can be used to combine enchantments from 2 items. The second item will lose its enchantment to fix the first. The items used must be the same for this to work, e.g. 2 diamond swords. Place the item to be fixed in the first anvil slot, and the other item in the second slot. The fixed item will then appear in the output slot. This will also cost you experience points.

COMBINING WITH AN ENCHANTED BOOK

You can find enchanted books in chests within strongholds, dungeons, jungle temples, desert temples, mineshafts and villages. You can also buy them with emeralds from NPC (Non-Player Character) village librarians, or make them on an enchantment table. To enchant an item, place the book in the sacrifice slot of your anvil and add the item to be enchanted.

ASKING A PRIEST VILLAGER

A priest villager will sometimes agree to enchant items, for a fee of emeralds. Just put the item and the requested amount of emeralds in the priest's trading slots and the enchanted item will appear in the output square. This won't even cost you any experience points. Brilliant!

POTIONS

Potions are drinkable items that have either a positive or negativ effect on a player. When used correctly, potions can really give you the upper hand in combat, so take some time to learn the basics.

BREWING STAND RECIPE

First, craft a brewing stand from a blaze rod and cobblestone. This is tricky, because blaze rods are only dropped by blazes (creatures found in or near Nether fortresses in the Nether). Eek! See pages 24–29 for how to survive in the Nether.

CAULDRON RECIPE

Next, you'll need to craft a cauldron from 7 iron ingots.

BUCKET RECIPE

Craft a bucket, fill it with water, then use it to fill the cauldron.

GLASS BOTTLE RECIPE

Craft glass bottles from glass blocks. 3 glass blocks will give you 3 bottles.

TIP: If you're going to get serious about potions, you'll need to set yourself up with a state-of-the-art potions lab, like this one. Find a suitable spot in your home, base or fort and fill it with all the necessary equipment and ingredients.

Fill 3 glass bottles with water from the cauldron and place 1 in each slot on your brewing stand.

AWKWARD POTION RECIPE

NETHER WART

3 bottles of awkward potion can be made by adding Nether wart to the top of your brewing stand. Nether wart can be found near to staircases in Nether fortresses. Awkward potion doesn't do anything on its own, but when combined with others it creates useful potions. Awkward, eh?

DID YOU KNOW? Awkward potion can be used as a base potion for all positive potions. Make sure you have a good supply of Nether wart at all times so that you're always ready to brew up a new batch.

HELPFUL POTIONS

Helpful potions have a positive or helpful effect when used. Once made, you can select a potion in your hotbar and use it to drink it. You will need 4 basic ingredients:

 Blaze powder: made from a blaze rod, dropped by blazes in the Nether

 Magma cream: dropped by magma cubes in the Nether or crafted from blaze powder and a slimeball

 Ghast tear: dropped by ghasts when killed

 Sugar: crafted from sugar cane

POTION OF STRENGTH

Made from awkward potion plus blaze powder, this potion will increase the amount of combat damage you can inflict on players or mobs.

BLAZE POWDER
+
AWKWARD POTION

BLAZE POWDER RECIPE

Place a blaze rod in your crafting grid to create blaze powder.

POTION OF HEALING

Made from awkward potion plus glistering melon, this potion will help you heal when you've been injured by restoring 4 health points per potion.

GLISTERING MELON
+
AWKWARD POTION

GLISTERING MELON RECIPE

A melon slice and 8 golden nuggets will make a glistering melon.

POTION OF SWIFTNESS

Made from awkward potion plus sugar, this potion will help you move more quickly, jump further and see further.

SUGAR RECIPE

Simply add sugar cane to your crafting grid to make sugar.

SUGAR

+

AWKWARD POTION

POTION OF INVISIBILITY

Made from awkward potion plus a golden carrot (to make potion of night vision), plus fermented spider eye (see next page), this will make the drinker invisible.

GOLDEN CARROT RECIPE

You'll need 8 golden nuggets and 1 carrot to make a golden carrot.

GOLDEN CARROT

+

FERMENTED SPIDER EYE

+

AWKWARD POTION

POTION OF REGENERATION

Made from awkward potion plus a ghast tear, this potion restores 18 health points over time by regenerating 1 health point per 2.5 seconds.

GHAST TEAR

+

AWKWARD POTION

HARMFUL POTIONS

You can use spider eyes and fermented spider eyes to create harmful potions to throw at your opponents. (See splash potions on the opposite page.) Spider eyes can be obtained by killing spiders or cave spiders, and may also be dropped by witches.

FERMENTED SPIDER EYE RECIPE

1 fermented spider eye can be crafted from a spider eye, a mushroom and sugar. Yuck. Do not mistake this for a tasty snack.

POTION OF HARMING

You can make this in two ways: potion of healing plus fermented spider eye, or potion of poison plus fermented spider eye. It will inflict 6 damage points on your opponent.

FERMENTED SPIDER EYE
+
POTION OF HEALING/POISON

POTION OF POISON

Made from awkward potion plus spider eye, this potion will poison the drinker for 22 seconds. The player loses 1 health point every 1.25 seconds until the poison wears off but the effect will stop when a player only has 1 health point remaining.

SPIDER EYE
+
AWKWARD POTION

POTION OF WEAKNESS

You can make this in two ways: potion of strength plus fermented spider eye or potion of regeneration plus fermented spider eye. This potion will reduce your opponent's melee/close-quarters attack strength by half for 1 minute 30 seconds.

FERMENTED SPIDER EYE

+

POTION OF STRENGTH/ REGENERATION

POTION OF SLOWNESS

Made in two ways: potion of fire resistance plus fermented spider eye or potion of swiftness plus fermented spider eye. This potion will reduce your opponent's walking ability to a crawl and reduce the distance they can jump for 1 minute 30 seconds.

FERMENTED SPIDER EYE

+

POTION OF FIRE RESISTANCE/ SWIFTNESS

SPLASH POTIONS

splash potion is a potion that can be thrown. You can turn any brewable otion into a splash potion simply by combining it with gunpowder. Brewing otions that have negative effects with gunpowder create splash potions that n be used as weapons against your opponents. Once brewed, place them your hotbar and hit the use item button to throw them at your opponents.

POISON   WEAKNESS   SLOWNESS   HARMING

PLAYER VERSUS PLAYER

Player versus player, or PVP, is a mode of multiplayer gameplay where you can battle against other players. You can tackle your opponents alone, or break off into teams. It's loads of fun!

ORGANISED

Organised PVP refers to PVP that you have chosen to participate in. If you join a dedicated PVP server or organise a PVP game with your friends, you can be said to be playing organised PVP. Many organised PVP games are set in specially built arenas. These are usually constructed in Creative mode, then the host changes the game type to Survival and opens the server to other players.

UNORGANISED

Unorganised PVP refers to occasions when you are attacked unexpectedly. Picture the scene: you're wandering happily through a forest, minding your own business, when another player hits you from behind with an enchanted diamond sword, killing you in a matter of moments. That's unorganised PVP. Talk about getting stabbed in the back!

MULTIPLAYER BY PAUL SOARES JR

PAUL SOARES JR: Paul is a Minecraft expert and was the first person to make Minecraft tutorials for YouTube. His debut video, How to Survive Your First Night, aired in 2010 and he has over 800,000 subscribers. Check out his channel for more combat tips!
youtube.com/paulsoaresjr

Playing Minecraft with your friends and family is great fun. You can help each other survive, team up on epic adventures, share creative builds and pull silly pranks! The possibilities are endless and all you need is a few other players and a way to connect to each other.

To play multiplayer on the Pocket Edition, your device will need to have a wifi signal, and will need to be 'visible' to other devices in the local area. Select multiplayer, then either start a new game and wait for friends to find you, or select join game and search for your friends.

If you want to play in multiplayer mode on the Xbox 360 Edition, you'll need Xbox live gold membership. You can then play with up to 8 other people, but you won't be able to access servers set up for the PC/Mac Edition. You can also try playing in split-screen mode with 3 other players on the same Xbox.

MULTIPLAYER
FOR PC/MAC EDITION

Playing multiplayer on the PC/Mac Edition is loads of fun, as you can play with much larger groups of people. You have three options:

1. START YOUR OWN DEDICATED SERVER

SEMI-ADVANCED GEEKINESS REQUIRED

A dedicated server is a specialised Minecraft server programme that runs on a computer and allows others to connect to it from just about anywhere in the world. This computer is called the host and you need to give your Internet IP Address to the people you have allowed to play on it. The host computer should be fairly modern to provide the best possible playing experience for everyone.

You can download the Minecraft server programme for free from the official Minecraft website (minecraft.net) and follow the installation instructions provided.

2. OPEN A SINGLE-PLAYER WORLD IN LAN WORLD MODE

BASIC COMPUTER SKILLS REQUIRED

If you have more than one computer at home you can use the Open to LAN feature (already built into Minecraft) to play with others on a single-player world. This is called a LAN (local area network) world and it's fairly simple to get one up and running. Here's the scoop:

1. Open a single-player world map and press the escape key.

2. Click the Open to LAN button.

3. Choose the Player Settings for this session, i.e. Game Mode and Allow Cheats.

4. Click Start LAN World.

Now, at the other computers on your local network, run Minecraft, choose Multiplayer, and your LAN World should appear. Select it, hit the Join Server button and let the games begin!

3. PLAY ON A DEDICATED ONLINE SERVER OR NETWORK

A ZOMBIE PIGMAN COULD DO IT

If you don't want to run your own server and don't mind playing with strangers, you can join an existing online server. Just click Multiplayer, Add Server, and enter the server address. That's the easy part.

The hard part is deciding which servers to add! There are thousands to choose from and each has its own set of rules, style of play and players. Try searching an online database such as minecraftservers.net for options. Many server operators advertise on popular Minecraft forums like minecraftforum.net and punchwood.com in order to recruit new players.

Remember, these sites aren't monitored by Mojang or Egmont so enter at your own risk. (See page 2 for our 'stay safe online' policy.)

Holiday event on Paulsoaresjr's private family server.

PRE-BATTLE CHECKLIST

Want to stay alive for as long as possible during organised PVP? Then you've got to be smart and get organised. Use this PVP checklist when preparing for battle.

 TIP: Create a system for your inventory, so that all food items are stored in one area, weapons in another, potions in another and so on. This will help you quickly transfer them to your hotbar in the middle of a battle.

Check

Full set of armour (iron at minimum) with an enchantment like protection or unbreaking

At least 2 swords with enchantments like sharpness, smite and knockback

An enchanted bow with at least 20 arrows

TNT

A lava bucket

A water bucket

Flint and steel

Splash potion of poison

Splash potion of weakness

Splash potion of harming

Potion of invisibility

Potion of healing

Potion of regeneration

Mushroom soup (see page 55)

Cooked steak

Golden apples, which not only restore food points but also give you Regeneration II for 5 seconds and Absorption for 2 minutes.

When playing PVP, make sure you've stored all your valuables in a chest in your base. DO NOT take them with you or you'll end up donating them to the player who finishes you off. Hide your chest under the floor to make it more difficult for raiders to find.

BATTLE STRATEGY

An experienced warrior knows that battle is all about strategy. It's not just about blowing people up – it's about planning your actions in advance and using your brain to gain the upper hand.

You could try running straight into the middle of a battle, hitting out at everyone and everything, but you'll be more successful if you try using these tips instead:

Craft a map as soon as you can to keep track of your location, as well as other players. Head for higher ground so you can see further and pounce on players below you.

Find a suitable spot for your base and get building. Try to position it away from other players. Sky bases and underground bases are the most difficult for your opponents to locate. Build your base from the strongest substance you can lay your hands on. Obsidian is best!

Approach your opponents from behind to give you the element of surprise, then use the strafing technique to circle them, making it more difficult for them to target you.

Keep your hand empty until face to face with an opponent, then select your weapon. This will lull them into a false sense of security. Try to get the first hit in, so that your opponent's health points are immediately depleted.

If you can force your opponent into water their movement will be slowed, giving you an advantage.

Sprinting at your enemy and hitting them, also known as sprint hitting, will enable you to knock them back further. Try block hitting (hitting and blocking at the same time). This allows you to deal damage to your opponent whilst taking less in return. Also, hit your opponent whilst jumping to deal more damage. This is called a critical hit.

Try mushroom souping! Save a sword in the first slot of your hotbar and mushroom stew/soup in the other 8. When your health has decreased to half mid-battle, block hit whilst simultaneously eating your stew. This allows you to regenerate health.

FORT BATTLEGROUND
BY FYREUK

Now that you're learning the Way of the Warrior, it's time to make a battleground on which to test out your new combat skills! A fort is the perfect setting for that epic battle you've been planning.

This fort, made by FyreUK, is an impressive battleground that includes many effective features. Turn the page to see how to create some of these features

FYREUK: Build team FyreUK specialise in constructing enormous, highly detailed builds in Minecraft. The sheer scale of some of these creations defies belief. Check out their YouTube channel for videos: **youtube.com/fyreuk**

FORT FEATURES

ARROW-FILLED DISPENSERS

Have you spotted the dispensers on the second level of the tower? They're filled with arrows and they face the entrances. Pressure plates behind allow you to activate them. Now you can fire arrows at attacking players while remaining under cover. (See page 11 for the dispenser recipe.)

SOUL SAND TRAP

Add soul sand to slow players down in open areas (this can be found in the Nether). You can place it sporadically, giving skilled players a chance to jump through it, or you can create a solid layer, forcing players to travel around it.

A traditional castle moat would be filled with water, but where's the fun in that? Fill it with lava instead and your opponents won't stand a chance. You'll need a few buckets of lava to fill a moat of this size. Keep placing the lava until the moat fills up.

CACTI MOAT

Alternatively, fill your moat with cacti, placed as closely together as possible. You could create a hidden entrance to the fort as a reward for any players who manage to weave through.

TIP: Be careful when using lava if you have a wooden drawbridge or walls – you do not want to be known as The Player Who Burnt Down Their Own Fort. Always keep a water bucket in your hotbar for emergencies.

LONG DROP TRAP
BY CNB MINECRAFT

This trap is invisible and virtually impossible to escape from! What looks like an innocent iron door with pressure plates is actually a trap that can send the player falling as far as the bedrock layer.

CONSTRUCTION MATERIALS

CNB MINECRAFT: Nick Farwell, AKA CNB Minecraft, is a redstone wizard. He can build everything from digital clocks to mob traps.

1

You'll need a regular doorway for this trap. Once finished, it should consist of a single door with a pressure plate on either side, but don't place the pressure plates yet, as you're about to dig a very deep hole!

2

Dig your pit directly in front of the door, at least 20 blocks deep. Remember the Number One Rule: never dig straight down. Dig a 2 x 1 hole so you can see what you're digging into whilst standing on the other block.

LONG DROP TRAP
... CONTINUED

3

Clear a 4 x 2 x 3 block space to the side of the door for the redstone circuit that will power the trap. At the top of the cleared area, place a single sticky piston facing in towards the pit. Repeat at the bottom and place a block in front of each piston.

4

Make sure the block in front of the top piston is the same as the rest of the ground so that it blends in. Place a blue wool block between 2 sticky pistons. Place a redstone torch on the left side of the blue wool block, then place a regular block above the torch and a single piece of redstone dust below it. The redstone torch will power both pistons so that they are pushed out.

5

Add a single regular piston facing the opposite way to the other 2, on the right-hand side of the blue wool block. Place another piece of redstone dust behind the regular piston.

6 Fill in the rest of the pit, then cover up the top with your wall and place your pressure plates on either side of the door. The only part of the trap now visible at ground level is a single side of the top piston. In most cases the doorway will be part of a wall, so it will be covered up completely. The next person who tries to enter is going to get a shock, and a very long drop ...

EXPLODING TREE TRAP
BY CNB MINECRAFT

This simple, classic trap is great fun for playing tricks on you
friends on multiplayer servers. The masterstroke is that it relie
merely on other players' fundamental need to gather wood. Geniu

The trap works by triggering TNT when a
player attempts to harvest the bottom
of a tree trunk. It's up to you
how much TNT you use, but
the 12 blocks shown here are
more than enough to cause
some serious damage!

CONSTRUCTION
MATERIALS

12	1	4	1	4

1

Choose a tree. Any type will work, but this example uses an oak tree. Pick a tree that is likely to be chopped down, e.g. one near to another player's base.

2

Dig out an area under the tree for the TNT and the activation circuit. It will need to be 2 blocks deep, 5 wide and 5 long, with the tree trunk positioned centrally.

3

Remove the bottom tree trunk block and place a single piece of redstone dust directly below the tree, then surround it with blue wool blocks as shown. Place a lever on the underside of the next trunk block, then flip it to the on position. The lever will provide power for the redstone dust.

EXPLODING TREE TRAP
... CONTINUED

4

Place redstone torches on the outer side of each wool block. These will activate the TNT when the lever is knocked off the trunk.

5

Now for the fun part – let's add the TNT! This build has 3 blocks of TNT in each corner of the pit.

6

Finally, cover the whole pit with dirt blocks (or any block that blends in with the terrain) to hide it.

7

Now all you have to do is wait for another player to undertake a spot of tree-chopping!

TNT CANNON
BY CNB MINECRAFT

This large cannon is powered by TNT and also fires TNT blocks. causes epic levels of destruction and can be used to great effect a a weapon, especially if you want to blow up an enemy base.

CONSTRUCTION
MATERIALS

1

Build a U-shaped frame using wool blocks and dispensers, 1 block above the ground. It should be 6 blocks long and 3 wide, and the dispensers should be facing in towards the centre of the U shape.

2

Add 3 wool blocks to the front of the U shape as shown. These will help guide the TNT cannonball. Now add a final dispenser, facing towards the column of wool blocks as shown.

TNT CANNON
... CONTINUED

Place 3 light green wool blocks in the centre of the U shape to create the cannon bed. They should sit on the ground, 1 block lower than the blue wool blocks.

Place a fence post and a pressure plate at the front of the cannon. Add water to the central bed, placing it at the back so that it runs towards the pressure plate.

Run redstone dust over the top of the first 2 dispensers along the side of the cannon. (PC/Mac users will need to hold shift and then right-click to place redstone dust on top of the dispensers.) Then place a pink wool block above the third dispenser and put a stone button on the side of it.

6

Place 6 repeaters in the positions shown. Make sure the repeaters point the right way – study this image carefully. Set each repeater to a 4-tick delay except for the one pointing into the lone dispenser. This should be on a 2-tick delay. Finally, add 2 pieces of redstone dust as shown to connect everything.

7

Now fill all 4 dispensers with TNT and give it a try!

HOW TO BUILD
AN EPIC BASE

Your base should be as secure as possible to keep you and your possessions safe. But if you want it to be truly epic you'll need to build something that looks intimidating enough to send your enemies running for the hills. Follow these tips to create a seriously epic base!

LOCATION
Position your base on high ground, not at the bottom of a hill. This will give you an advantage over approaching enemies as you'll be able to see them coming. It also prevents them taking you by surprise from above.

MATERIALS
Build your base out of Nether brick. This tells your enemies that you've survived the Nether long enough to collect a lot of resources, so they might think twice about taking you on. Also, Nether brick is immune to fire making it a good choice for a combat zone.

FLAMING NETHERRACK
Use netherrack to create floating blocks of fire at each side of the entrance. This is another great intimidation tactic – you've been to the Nether AND you like fire? Clearly you're not to be messed with.

LAVA

Use lava wherever you can. To create streams running down the side of your base, place 4 blocks of Nether brick in a cross shape, then use a lava bucket to place lava in the centre. This will create an infinite source of lava.

SECURITY

Use iron bars instead of glass for windows. They're more difficult to destroy than glass, and you'll still be able to see your enemies coming. Iron bars are technically solid blocks so arrows can't pass through the gaps which means you can stand behind them safely.

IRON BAR RECIPE

16

16 iron bars can be crafted from 6 iron ingots.

DOOR TRAP

Create a trapped door to trick any raiders who actually make it to the entrance. See pages 60–63 for an awesome long drop trap.

RAIDING A BASE

Raiding an enemy base is a lot of fun. It provides you with more resources, and also reduces your opponents' capabilities, making them less of a threat. Here's how to do it right.

TIMING
Attack at night. When raiding an enemy base, the darkness is your friend.

RECON
Observe the area before you attack. See who's there and how to use the terrain to your advantage.

TAG TEAM
Recruit a friend to help you – two players are better than one.

TOOLS
Take the strongest tool you can. An enchanted diamond pickaxe is ideal as it will allow you to mine tough blocks like obsidian the quickest. And remember to take spares.

YOUR ENEMY'S ENEMY
If there are any creepers about, lure them towards the base. They might just help you blow up the outer wall, free of charge.

SPLASH POTIONS
Take splash potions to use against your opponents in case they emerge.

HEALTH
Bring food to replenish your health and hunger bars.

TESTING YOUR SKILLS ON A
CUSTOM MAP BY FYREUK

now you've mastered the art of combat, it's time to pick up your sword, put on your helmet and find out if you're the best warrior Minecraft has ever seen! And we've got the perfect map for you.

This is Remnant – one of FyreUK's custom Survival Games maps. Survival Games isn't just about battling each other, it's also about surviving the landscape. Within the Remnant map you'll find small villages, temples and hidden areas containing chests filled with useful items. Your goal is to collect these items, battle the other players on the map and win.

CHESTS
Finding chests quickly and grabbing the useful items will give you an advantage over other players.

CRAFTING RECIPES
Remember your crafting recipes, particularly the sword, bow, arrow and armour recipes. A bow and arrow can be particularly useful on a large map as you'll be able to take out your enemies from a distance.

SNEAKING
Use the sneak function to crouch and hide your name from other nearby players (your name appears over your head in multiplayer and can be seen through blocks).

VALUABLE ITEMS

When playing the Remnant map, you won't have to run far from the start point to find valuable items. The temple in the centre has many hidden pathways and a complex, maze-like hallway system inside, and many a treasure can be found there.

CORRIDORS

Be wary of small enclosed spaces like corridors as you may find yourself cornered with no way out. A lot of early battles happen in small spaces.

PC/Mac users: want to try the Remnant map for yourself? You can download it from minecraft.egmont.co.uk

Check out PlanetMinecraft (www.planetminecraft.com) for more downloadable custom maps.

(See page 2 for our 'Stay safe online' policy.)

ACHIEVEMENTS

Minecraft takes note of your achievements when you're playing the PC/Mac Edition or the Xbox 360 Edition. Here are some key combat achievements to aim for.

PC/MAC EDITION:

 TIME TO STRIKE!
Use planks and sticks to make a sword.

 MONSTER HUNTER
Attack and destroy a monster.

 SNIPER DUEL
Kill a skeleton or wither skeleton with an arrow from more than 50 metres.

 WE NEED TO GO DEEPER
Build a portal to the Nether.

 RETURN TO SENDER
Destroy a ghast with a fireball.

 THE END?
Locate the End.

 THE END
Defeat the ender dragon.

 OVERKILL
Deal 8 hearts of damage in a single hit.

 THE BEGINNING?
Spawn the wither.

 THE BEGINNING
Kill the wither.

XBOX 360 EDITION:

TIME TO STRIKE!
Use planks and sticks to make a sword.

MONSTER HUNTER
Attack and destroy a monster.

INTO THE NETHER
Build a portal to the Nether.

USEFUL LINKS

Congratulations! You've made it to the end of the Minecraft Combat Handbook, which means you're now a fearsome warrior. Your enemies had better beware!

Check out this list of useful websites. They'll really help you take your Minecrafting to the next level.

Official Minecraft website:
www.minecraft.net

Mojang Team's YouTube channel:
www.youtube.com/teammojang

Official Mojang website:
www.mojang.com

The official Minecraft Twitter page:
https://twitter.com/mojangteam

The Minecraft wiki:
www.minecraftwiki.net

Jeb's official Twitter page:
https://twitter.com/jeb_

The official Facebook page:
www.facebook.com/minecraft

Egmont's Minecraft website:
minecraft.egmont.co.uk

These other Minecraft sites, not monitored by Mojang or Egmont. Enter at your own risk!

Detailed server information:
minecraftservers.net

Texture packs:
www.minecrafttexturepacks.com

Minecraft on Reddit:
www.reddit.com/r/Minecraft/

Paul Soares Jr's YouTube channel:
www.youtube.com/paulsoaresjr

FyreUK's YouTube channel:
www.youtube.com/fyreuk

(Turn to page 2 for our 'Stay safe online' policy.)